Bitcoin:
The Ultimate Cryptocurrency

Digital Money Guide

Author: R.J. Simmons

All Rights Reserved.

No part of this publication may be reproduced in any form or by any means, including scanning, photocopying, or otherwise without prior written permission of the copyright holder.

Copyright © 2016

Published by:

R.J. Simmons and Random Technologies

4409 HOFFNER AVENUE, 347

Belle Isle, FL 32812

www.SparrowPublications.com

Table of Contents

Disclaimer 1

Chapter 1 - Money, As We Know It 3
    The Real Value of Money 4
    Banks Explained 6

Chapter 2 - Cryptocurrency and Bitcoins 9
    Digital Currencies – Kinds and Examples 9
    Bitcoins and Other Cryptocurrencies 10
    The Increasing Popularity of Bitcoins 12
    The Bitcoin Advantage 14
    Uses of Bitcoins 17

Chapter 3 - Starting with Bitcoins 19
    Acquiring Bitcoins - The Complete Guide 19
    Pricing of Bitcoins 24
    Storage of Bitcoins - Different Wallets and Their Uses 24
    Choosing the Right Wallet 33
    Bitcoin ATMs 34
    Quick Recap 35

Chapter 4 - Bitcoin Transaction Process 39
    The Problem of Double Spending 39
    A Sample Bitcoin Transaction 40
    Nuances of the Transaction 41
    Blockchain 43
    Miners and Mining 43
    Pooling 46
    Going Solo or Pooling 46
    Getting Started With Mining 47
    Getting Started With Pooling 51
    Quick Recap 52

Chapter 5 - Selling and Trading Bitcoins 55
    Trading and Selling Bitcoins.. 55
    Conversion Back Into Dollars 56
    Good Trading Practices 57
    Legality of the Currency 58
    Taxation and Government Claims on Bitcoin Income 58

Chapter 6 - Concerns and Risks 61
    Common Concerns 61
    Potential Risks 63

Chapter 7 - Conclusion... 65

Disclaimer

The author has made every attempt to be as accurate and complete as possible in the creation of this publication/PDF, however he / she does not warrant or represent at any time that the contents within are accurate due to the rapidly changing nature of the Internet. The author assumes no responsibility for errors, omissions, or contrary interpretation of the subject matter herein. Any perceived slights of specific persons, peoples, or organizations other published materials are unintentional and used solely for educational purposes only.

This information is not intended for use as a source of legal, business, accounting or financial advice. All readers are advised to seek services of competent professionals in the legal, business, accounting, and finance field. No representation is made or implied that the reader will do as well from using the suggested techniques, strategies, methods, systems, or ideas; rather it is presented for news value only.

The author does not assume any responsibility or liability whatsoever for what you choose to do with this information. Use your own judgment. Consult appropriate professionals before starting a business or making ANY investment. Any perceived remark, comment or use of organizations, people mentioned and any resemblance to characters living, dead or otherwise, real or fictitious does not mean that they support this content in any way but is provided for news value / information only.

There are no guarantees of income made, and understand investment is often very risky, especially cryptocurrencies. NO PROMISES ARE MADE of any kind and all information provided is for information value only!

Readers are cautioned to reply on their own judgment about their individual circumstances to act accordingly. By reading any document, the reader agrees that under no circumstances is the author responsible for any losses, direct or indirect, that are incurred as a result of use of the information contained within this document, including - but not limited to errors, omissions, or inaccuracies.

Buying, selling and trading cryptocurrencies is inherently risky, especially if you base any reliance on this as a means to making money.

This guide is for basic information only and you must do your own research, investigation and proof of what I say in this guide is viable for you and your unique situation.

While many cryptocurrency trades happen daily, and the vast majority of trades are satisfactory as an investment and safety vehicle, moneymaking is not typically the reason.

This guide was written with the express purpose of giving you the information you need to make intelligent decisions as to whether or not you wish to consider crypto currencies is a superior and safer method to current financial institutions, such as large banks.

Most people invest in cryptocurrencies as a security and privacy factor. While you can and eventually should be able to make additional money, this is by no means guarantee in any way.

Please use this information wisely. Check with professionals in investments and seek financial consultation as I cannot guarantee anything that you choose to do, as I have no way of supervising how you use this information.

Chapter 1 - Money, As We Know It

Have you ever wondered the importance of money in our life?

How *difficult* would it be to live a decent life without the dollars in your pocket and a credit card in your wallet? How *incredibly hard* would it be to live life?

There are no two ways about the fact that money plays a significant role in your life. Money is used to not just to live, but to live conveniently and luxuriously. All of this begs the question - *what exactly is money?*

Before that question is answered, let us take a trip down some centuries.

From the beginning of time, humans realized that they can't do everything themselves. Either they can grow wheat or rice in the limited areas of their field. So they realized that they can exchange what they have for what they want with others. In the early times, before the society had *a medium of exchange* to rely on, people used to barter. One goat for a horse, one bag of rice for a bushel of wheat, a bottle of milk for a bottle of oil and so on.

This was all based on the importance of the objects for them and importance of anything is always relative. For a trade or an exchange to happen, each party must be interested enough in the other party's product to go for it. This was highly inconvenient and caused a lot of chaos and conflict. What if you want oil but don't have milk for it? Unless you want to go to the person selling wheat and willing to exchange your rice for wheat, then go to the person who is selling sugar and is willing to exchange it for rice and then go back to the person selling oil and give him sugar to obtain oil. This process complicates the exchange process, doing the exact opposite of what it was started for.

Thus came the need for a neutral medium of exchange. Let us say, A wants oil and has wheat whereas B has oil but wants milk. A can just hand over the agreed upon units of the medium of exchange (clay tablets, gold, coins, paper notes, digital currency) and get the oil from B. B can then use those units of exchange to buy milk for himself. If A hands over 2 units of the medium of exchange for the oil and B hands over 1 of those 2 units for buying milk, B will still have 1 unit left for future purchases. Not only was a neutral medium of exchange easily divisible unlike a goat, it was also easily stored for future uses, unlike milk which will perish in a day or two.

The benefits of shifting to a neutral medium were immense and the society naturally evolved to it from the clunky barter system and the first form of money was born.

In very simple terms, that's what money[1] is - a medium of exchange.

But in addition to a medium of exchange, money is also a store of value. The value that you provided to other members of the society doesn't have to be encashed right that moment. It can be stored for use in future. If you store USD $1 million in a bank, it will still retain its value after a year. This wasn't possible with commodities like milk and groceries.

The Real Value of Money

When B agreed to take 2 units of money from A, he placed the value of the note, coin, and clay tablet to be worth the oil he sold. But technically, the piece of paper is worthless, unless he can use it to buy milk. One very important fact about money is that its value depends on the value that you place on it. The money, as a medium of exchange, is useful only if the entire society agrees to use it.

Eventually instead of money deriving its value from the goods and services, it came to be the other way around. Money grew to become a unit of account - the prices of goods and services came to be measured in terms of money required to buy a certain quantity of them.

Let us imagine a hypothetical scenario. If one fine day you woke up to find out that the billion dollars in your bank are not being accepted anymore by anybody for anything, what would you be able to do?

---

1 For the purpose of this chapter, money means notes, coins as well as bank money

Chapter 1: Money, As We Know It

Let us say, you have a billion dollars in your bank this second, you are rich and you can buy anything in the world. So you decide to buy yourself a nice car. After careful considerations, you decide on a Lamborghini because the car should measure up to your status. You go to a car showroom to buy it, only the dealer asks you to pay in gold. He says he doesn't accept dollars anymore.[2] You go to another one muttering under your breath. The other dealer also refuses to accept the payment in dollars. What would you do? In a situation like this, even though you have a billion dollars in your bank account, the money is essentially worthless.

This example signifies that money is only valuable to the extent, we as a society, put a value on it. If the society decides to not put its faith in the current system of money, the money becomes essentially useless.

But the money is supposed to have some intrinsic value. Even if the society has refused to accept the dollars that you want to pay them, can't you still go to the bank and ask them to give you gold or any other useful asset in exchange for the billion dollars. Well, no.

When we first started with money, we used coins made from precious metals like gold, silver and copper. That means, even if nobody accepts your money, you still have an equivalent value of precious resources in your possession, which can potentially be used for purchasing goods and services. During this phase, the value of the currency was backed by the precious metals used to make it.

We later transitioned to paper notes and coins, the value of which is definitely not contained in the material used to make them. When we first made paper money, it was decided that it would be backed by gold so that it is legitimate and *valuable* to the general populace that's using it.

But we transitioned from gold-backed currency, to what is called fiat currency.

Fiat currency is not backed by any real asset. That means you cannot go to the Federal Reserve and ask for gold in exchange for the billion dollars. The value of the current US dollars is derived not by the

---

2   This will not happen in the near future, it is illegal to not accept USD as a payment for goods and services in the US. Just think of it as a hypothetical scenario.

commodity value but by a rule of law where a particular currency unit has a certain value. This is decided by the central bank initially and the forces of demand and supply come into the picture later.

Because of the power vested in the hands of the central bank, it can choose to print more money at any time, devaluing the current money holders and making them poorer comparatively. That is because the more money there is in a system, the lesser its value. 100 dollars in a 10000 dollar ecosystem is 1% of the total, but only 0.5% in a 20000 dollar ecosystem.

Putting everything together, the value of money is derived from - value the society places on it, scarcity and desire to hold more money.

Banks Explained

There are two major kinds of banks in any economy - the central bank and the commercial banks. One of the major roles of any central bank is to stabilize the inflation level in an economy. The central bank achieves this by controlling the interest rates and money supply in the economy at a particular point in time.

At any point in time, the central banks can decide to lower or increase the interest rates and pump in or squeeze out liquidity from the system in order to maintain a general price level stability and growth conditions in the economy.

The central bank is also the *only* institution that has a hold over the money supply. That means it can authorize or de-authorize some payments, devalue or revalue the currency without the need of approval from the concerned participants i.e. people who are actually holding this money.

Because we use fiat currency[3], the central bank is no longer required to have a backing for the currency, which permits it to generate currency at the time and consisting of an amount of its choosing.

---

3 Fiat Currency is the currency which is not backed by equivalent amount of gold, forex or other assets

The central bank doesn't usually deal with the public directly. That role is played by the commercial banks. They take deposits from the public at a certain deposit rate and lend it to the public at a higher rate. They keep the margin.

In other words, commercial banks serve as financial intermediaries.

For example,

Q deposits his savings of 100 dollars in his bank account at 3%. P goes to the bank to get a loan of 100 dollars for 3 years for starting a new business venture at 4%. The bank uses Q's funds to loan P and earns 1% on that amount for acting as an intermediary.

Let us imagine another scenario where financial intermediaries are not used.

P can borrow from Q at 3.5%, instead of borrowing from the bank. He will save on bank's processing charges and other fees and Q will get a larger amount of interest than he gets by the bank. At the end of three years, he can return the principal to Q. Doesn't that make it a no-brainer? Well, not.

If all goes well, P can return the amount to Q. But what if the business never takes off and P doesn't have enough money to pay back to Q? He has essentially drowned Q's life savings. If Q doesn't have contacts in the local mafia, it may seem impossible to get back the savings. If P doesn't have any personal money at all, it will be very difficult to actually obtain the money back.

But not if the transaction was conducted through a bank. Even if P doesn't repay the loan, Q will still get his initial deposits as well as interest on the deposits. The commercial banks assume and therefore eliminate the counter-party risk.

> *The commercial banks act as financial intermediaries and assume the risk inherent in the transaction.*

If all the loans of the banks turn into bad debts (commonly called as Non-Performing Assets - NPAs), the bank will no longer be able to give the initial deposits back to its depositors. In other words, the bank will fail. Banks can fail, but central bank won't let that happen. The central bank will usually bail a bank account, in order to prevent a major shake-up.

Banks are, therefore, a very important engine for the growth of any economy. Money is at the heart of this growth. By providing financial intermediation services, banks help in credit creation. For this service, they charge various kinds of fees - transaction fees, processing charges, bank charges, ATM charges and so on.

In addition to helping in credit creation, banks also offer a way to transfer money from one account to another. Often the process of transfer, especially international transfers, is not at all transparent benefitting the banks at the cost of the account holders. The account holders have little knowledge about the nature and amount of the fee or the reasons for levy of other charges.

Add to this, the increasing usage of internet for making payments. Banks offer online transfers but this process is riddled with the same inefficiencies - translucent processes and exorbitant fees.

All of this called for a new kind of currency - a currency that could improve on these inefficiencies and make digital transactions a breeze.

Chapter 2 - Cryptocurrency and Bitcoins

This led to the rise of digital banking and virtual currency. Because these currencies could not successfully solve the problems, cryptocurrency was launched which seemed to be a viable solution, at least at the onset.

Digital Currencies – Kinds and Examples

Digital currency is one which is capable of being stored and transferred online, which implies any currency that can be expressed in binary form i.e. as a combination of 0s and 1s. Although it is distinct from physical currency yet it exhibits several similar properties. For instance, it can be used to pay for goods and services over the web.

US dollars used over the web are an example of a digital currency. US dollars can be used to pay for your burger if you physically visit the shop and you can also use the same US dollars to pay for the burger online using your credit card.

A digital currency can be easily converted into physical currency. Essentially all currencies like the US dollar, Australian dollar, Japanese Yen etc. have their digital counterparts today.

> *Digital currency is a currency which lives online.*

Virtual currency, as the name suggests, is 'virtual' i.e. something which doesn't exist in the real world. A subset of digital currency, virtual currency cannot be used to pay for goods or services, nor can it be converted into a real currency at any time whatsoever.

Virtual currencies are usually currencies that exist in game worlds or specific online shops. You buy virtual currency using a real currency like US dollars or earn them by participating in a game or winning a round of the game online. Virtual currencies are often controlled by a central authority, just like US dollars, usually the creators of the game or the online store.

> *Virtual currency is a currency which lives online and can't go back to the real world.*

Cryptocurrency is another subset of digital currency which means it is also stored online but is an improvement over the current currency systems. As the name suggests, cryptocurrency uses the principles of cryptography for creation and storage of currencies online. The use of cryptography ensures that the currency is safe from being counterfeited and the transfer of funds using this currency is secure.

Cryptocurrencies are not regulated by any central authority. The rate at which cryptocurrency will be produced is decided when the software is launched and the information is freely available to the public. It is produced, not by one department but by the people who are using the software.

The ledger of transactions done using cryptocurrency is maintained by public and is available to the public. The transactions done using cryptocurrency is not always completely anonymous, but mostly so.

> *Cryptocurrency is a currency which lives online, completely secure.*

Bitcoins and Other Cryptocurrencies

Bitcoin is the first cryptocurrency, created back in 2009. A bitcoin, like all forms of cryptocurrency, is a decentralized currency system which means that this medium of exchange is not controlled by any single party. The supply of the bitcoins is fixed at 21 million bitcoins and is not authorized by a centralized bank or a company.

Bitcoins were founded by a person or a group of people who went by the pseudonym of Satoshi Nakamoto. Satoshi Nakamoto published a paper on decentralized online currencies in October 2008 and launched a bitcoin software (referred to as a Bitcoin with a capital B) in January 2009 whose currency was bitcoins.

Bitcoin is, therefore, at the heart of cryptocurrency movement.

A number of other cryptocurrencies (collectively referred to as altcoins) were started after Bitcoin, and some of them have seen partial success but none have been able to match Bitcoin's place in the online world.

Dogecoin: Dogecoin was created by Oregon programmer Billy Markus as a fun substitute for bitcoins. It is usually used to tip others online. It is used as an online meme.

Initially the founders started with the plan of producing 100 billion dogecoins but later declared that dogecoins will be unlimited in number. Dogecoins are earned similarly as bitcoins, by mining.

As of June 2016, the price of a dogecoin is USD 0.00029.

Ether: Ether is the cryptocurrency which is built on its own blockchain platform called Ethereum. Ether has a variety of new features compared to bitcoins and is proving to be a serious competitor to bitcoins.

The New York Times described Ether as *"a single shared computer that is run by the network of users and on which resources are parceled out and paid for by Ether."*

Ethereum has the second largest market capitalization after Bitcoins.[4]

As of June 2016, the price of an Ethereum is USD 12.6007.

Litecoin: Litecoin was created by a former Google employee and is very similar to Bitcoin. The protocols are nearly identical, but litecoin transactions are processed every 2.5 minutes compared to 10 minutes it takes for bitcoin transactions to be processed. The total number of litecoins ever produces will also be four times the total number of bitcoins at 84 million litecoins.

As of June 2016, the price of a litecoin is USD 5.54.

---

4   Data from http://coinmarketcap.com/ accessed on June 14, 2016

The Increasing Popularity of Bitcoins

The most important thing for any currency, as we discussed in the previous chapter, is to be valuable. And the value of a currency depends on two factors - scarcity and the perceived value.

The central banks give the physical currency a perceived value in the economy. Because of the guarantee by the central bank and the government, the currency is legitimate in the eyes of the public.

But there is no such authority for bitcoins. Because some governments like China and Thailand put a ban on the use of bitcoins, it suffered some damage to its image as a legitimate brand. Recently the *seeming* value of bitcoins is on an increase because of the kind of transactions that have happened using bitcoins.

Increasing acceptance of bitcoins

The first bitcoin transaction took place in May 2010 when a Florida programmer Laszlo Hanyecz offered 10000 bitcoins to anyone who buys him pizzas. When the transaction took place, bitcoins were recently launched and the price of 1 bitcoin was equal to USD 0.03. A citizen of England took Laszlo for his offer and ordered him a USD 25 pizza.

This transaction marks a significant shift in the Bitcoin economy. Before this, nobody had even anticipated that bitcoins could be used to buy real goods and services.

Had Laszlo not used those 10000 bitcoins then, he would be worth USD 73 million as of June 2016. But on the other hand, if he hadn't done the transaction then, in most likelihood, bitcoins will not be as valuable today.

In 2013, a company called Robocoin installed an ATM machine in Vancouver, Canada for the first time ever. It was installed right outside a coffee shop that accepted bitcoins as a valid form of payment. The ATM kiosk allowed users to deposit money and converted it into bitcoins as well as withdraw bitcoins as physical cash.

Chapter 2: Cryptocurrency and Bitcoins

On the first day, the ATM saw transactions for more than USD 10000[5] and crossed the USD 1 million mark in the first month.[6]

This not only helped in legitimizing the currency in the eyes of the public but also helped in injecting a certain amount of liquidity in the Bitcoin network. It helped increase the user base of bitcoins as well, as more than 50% of the people using the ATM in the first month were new users.[7] After the success of Bitcoin ATMs in Vancouver, Robocoin planned to install new Bitcoin ATMs in different locations in Canada and subsequently in other parts of the world.

There are 669 Bitcoin ATMs in the world as on June 2016 with the USA topping the list at 327 ATMs.[8]

The currency has now begun to gain increasing acceptance in the offline world as well. Two newlyweds in the USA decided to live only on items that could be bought using bitcoins. During this period, they travelled to places across the world including Stockholm, Berlin and Singapore. They lasted a hundred and one days, nearly three and a half months. They made a documentary about their journey.[9]

The fact that bitcoins can be used offline signals that the world has started placing some value on the currency. And we have already established the fact that money is worth what we believe it is worth.

Better Currency for Masses

Bitcoins were launched in the wake of the 2008 financial meltdown. This was exactly the time when people were losing faith in the modern system of currencies and monetary policy was deemed less efficient in stimulating the economy.

---

5   http://abcnews.go.com/Technology/bitcoin-atm-conducts-10000-worth-transactions-day/story?id=20730762
6   http://www.geekwire.com/2013/worlds-bitcoin-atm-exceeds-1m-transaction-volume-month/
7   http://www.geekwire.com/2013/worlds-bitcoin-atm-exceeds-1m-transaction-volume-month/
8   https://coinatmradar.com/charts/
9   http://lifeonbitcoin.com/

Bitcoins promised a newer better currency, which had absolutely zero strings attached to the central banks. Central banks don't control the currency or have the power to take any decisions related to the currency.

Because the currency was deregulated and decentralized, the value of the currency would depend on demand and supply of the currency. There would be no financial intermediaries for carrying out the transaction, everything would happen in a public ledger using a blockchain. Intermediaries usually become the pain points and blockchains have eliminated the need for bitcoins.

Another point in favor of the bitcoins is the scarcity of bitcoins. Only a finite amount (21 million bitcoins) of it will ever be produced. The scarcity of bitcoins has led to the belief that the wealth contained in bitcoins will not be eroded over time. The bitcoins will just become more and more valuable. Also, the bitcoins can easily be exchanged across geographies without the need for financial intermediaries like banks.

The fact that the currency wouldn't lose its value and could be easily exchanged online contributed to its initial appeal. And after the increasing acceptance of bitcoins in the real world, the currency has started becoming more and more valuable.

The Bitcoin Advantage

With the increasing popularity of bitcoins, comes even greater advantages because of the pros of using bitcoins for carrying out transactions. There are certain characteristics of bitcoins and the transactions carried out using bitcoins that make them a viable currency to transact in.

Fast and Cheap

It can take days for a bank transaction to go through. When you issue a check, the bank reviews your account for funds and then transfer the amount to the person the money was intended for. An International wire transfer can take days for the money to transfer from one party to another.

Bitcoins transactions, on the other hand, are instantaneous transactions. Banks also charge fees for their services, which includes a transaction processing charge as well as a Foreign Exchange Conversion cost. Bitcoin transactions are almost free of fee charges.

Privately Owned

In the Republic of Cyprus, in 2013, there was a severe financial crisis where the bad debts ratio continued to increase and threatened to put the banking system in a bind. The bank had to be bailed out by the European Union with USD 13 million of assistance. Then in a shocking announcement, the European Union asked the depositors of the bank to bear USD 7.5 million of that amount.

Imagine you have an account in this bank and hold USD 100 in that account. After the announcement and decision, a certain amount will just be taken away from your hard-earned money.

Needless to say, this caused a huge unrest in the general population of Cyprus.

Anything remotely close cannot happen with bitcoins. Bitcoins are secure and free from control by any kind of central governments, making them your own money. This means no single authority can take it away from you legally or create financial scams by manipulating the flow of bitcoins.

Transparent, yet Anonymous

Bitcoins are nearly anonymous. Each person can hold as many bitcoin addresses as he wants, none of which are linked to any revealing personal information such as name, home address and country of residence.

However, the system is completely transparent. It uses a public ledger called blockchain. This means that the information about the number of bitcoins stored in any address is accessible to anybody with a workable internet connection. Because the public address is not linked to other information, the private information stays private.

Anybody can see your bitcoin wealth online, but nobody can know that the wealth belongs to you.

Secure

The most popular way of doing transactions online, the credit card, is a very insecure form of making payment. You part away with all the material information such as the credit card number, the CSV code and the expiry date on a web payment gateway. This information can easily be hacked and subsequently used by anyone to carry on fraudulent transactions. The lack of proper security is, in part, the reason why credit card information is stolen so often.

Bitcoins are secure. Once the transaction has taken place, it is impossible for the transaction to be called back. Also the transparent and very public system of using blockchain to validate the payment makes it more secure and less susceptible to fraud than other currencies.

The bitcoins don't require any secure information to be given away for any transaction. To achieve this, bitcoin protocol uses two kinds of keys - a public key and a private key. Whenever you transfer bitcoins to another account, you authorize the transaction by using a combination of your public key and your private key.

The method of using two keys ensures that your private key is confidential and is not accessible to be stolen.

Inflation-proof Currency

Fiat currency, which is controlled by the government, can be printed at will. This causes an increase in demand for goods and services, which results in an increase in prices and loss in value of the currency.

For example, A holds USD 100 in a USD 10000 economy. He currently has 1% of the wealth. Let us assume that the price of a mobile phone is USD 50, which makes it feasible for him to buy 2 phones.

Now, the government prints more currency and takes the total money supply in the economy to USD 15000. The phone will become costlier because more people now have the money to buy it. Let us say that the price of the phone increases to USD 75. Now A can buy 1.16 phones. Although he holds the same dollar value in absolute terms, he has *just* become poorer.

Because bitcoin currency is decentralized, privately owned and has a fixed number of units that will ever be in circulation, the currency is fairly resistant to inflation and a resultant loss in value.

Uses of Bitcoins

It may seem that bitcoins are just an internet fad with little acceptability and volatility, but it is not so. In fact, bitcoins can be used for a number of purposes:

Trading

Bitcoins can be used for trading, just like stocks. You can speculate on bitcoins just like you speculate on shares and options. Because bitcoin is a relatively new currency, the volatility is very high, which makes for quick cash. You can take your position in the beginning of the week and square it off at the end of the week.

Long-term Investment

A lot of people use bitcoins for long-term investment purpose, assuming that the currency is here to stay for the long term and eventually would provide good returns. You can buy a small amount of currency weekly till you have a reasonable amount. You can also club long-term investment with short-term trading by selling a small amount when the market picks up pace occasionally.

International Mode of Exchange

Bitcoins can also be used to quickly and painlessly transfer money across geographies. You don't need to store bitcoins for this purpose. When the need arises, you can convert your dollars into bitcoins and send them or receive them and convert them into dollars immediately.

Medium of Exchange

Bitcoins can also be used as a medium of exchange, which means you can use it to pay for goods and services. Many, albeit not a lot, merchants across the world accept bitcoins as payment.

Chapter 3 - Starting with Bitcoins

Bitcoins are a revolutionary currency which has the potential to change the way we hold and use our money. In the preceding chapters, we have talked about the characteristics of Bitcoin that make it a good investment opportunity.

In this chapter, we will talk about how to tap into the brilliant investment opportunity that bitcoins provide.

Acquiring Bitcoins - The Complete Guide

The first step to investing in bitcoins is to acquire them. Bitcoins are different from normal currency and hence are acquired in slightly different ways. There are four major ways of acquiring bitcoins:

- Mining
- Over The Counter exchanges
- Bitcoin exchanges
- Payment for goods and services
- Mining

Mining is the process of using your computer and hardware capabilities to help authenticate the transactions and earn bitcoins as a fee. As the time passes, the process of mining becomes more difficult, requiring better equipment in exchange for comparatively lesser bitcoins. Despite this, mining remains a popular way to acquire bitcoins. We will discuss mining in detail in the next chapter.

This is the only way to acquire **new bitcoins** from the Bitcoin economy. The other three ways focus on purchasing the existing bitcoins already mined.

Over The Counter Exchange

Over The Counter or OTC exchange is an exchange of cash for bitcoins in a physical location. The users meet at a pre-decided location, where the buyer pays the seller the decided amount of cash and other requisite information for buying bitcoins.

Once the cash settlement has been done, the bitcoins are sent by the seller to the buyer's exchange account or the public bitcoin address. This is usually a quick and secure way of transacting and the bitcoins are transferred as speedily as 30 minutes.

OTC markets are generally used by power users to make transactions of large values for enhanced security and trust in the process.

Step 1: Find a counterparty to trade with.

Any trade transaction requires two parties who are *interested* in the transaction. An engaged counterparty can either be found with the help of traders and brokers or online through platforms like the Bitcoin OTC (https://bitcoin-otc.com) or the Deal Co (http://www.dealco.in/)

Step 2: Negotiate on terms and conditions.

The next step is to negotiate the best price. The party with more bargaining power may ask the other party to set a price and then accept, reject or increase it. This is a stage where an almost heated discussion happens on the value of bitcoins and other perks.

Step 3: Finalize the exchange.

Once the price has been finalized, the two parties meet and the seller transfers the bitcoin funds to the buyer's address after fulfillment of all formalities related to the sale.

Bitcoin Exchanges

Bitcoin exchanges are places where bitcoin users meet each other in order to sell or buy bitcoins. A lot of bitcoin exchanges double up as a wallet, providing its users a safe place to store their bitcoins.

Bitcoin exchanges help you exchange bitcoins without meeting the other party. They also eliminate counterparty risk i.e. the risk of the other party not honoring its commitment to buy or sell the decided number of bitcoins.

Exchanges are riddled with security concerns. One of the most popular Bitcoin exchange in its time, Mt. Gox declared itself bankrupt because of the number of bitcoins it lost during its lifetime. This incident shook the bitcoin user community who became wary of exchanges in general.

Using an exchange is a simple process.

Step 1: Select an exchange.

Because of security reasons and the different perks that each exchange provides, it becomes essential to choose the exchange carefully.

- Bitstamp - Bitstamp exchange (https://www.bitstamp.net/) boasts of being one of the first exchanges to be given a license by any government. Bitstamp secured a license from Luxembourg government. Connecting your bank account may take a few days depending on the bank.

- Coinbase - Coinbase exchange (https://www.coinbase.com/) is one of the most reputable exchanges in the Bitcoin community. One of the unique selling propositions of Coinbase exchange is the near instantaneous verification process of the bank account connected with the Bitcoin wallet.

- BTC-e – BTC-e (https://btc-e.com/) has established itself as one of the top bitcoins exchange platforms. It allows for automatic trading and instant withdrawal of coins. It also lets you withdraw coins into US dollars within 3 days.

Step 2: Connect your bank account.

Once you have finalized your exchange, you need to sign up for a new account at the exchange and connect your bank account to the exchange account. At a particular point of time, you will have two accounts - an exchange account and your bank account connected with the exchange account.

Step 3: Transfer funds and buy bitcoins.

The next step is to transfer funds from your bank account to your exchange account to enable buying of bitcoins. Depending on the exchange you have chosen, it may take anywhere between 10 minutes to 3 days for the connection to be approved by your local bank. After buying bitcoins, you can choose to keep your funds in the account or store them in a wallet.

Step 4: Start the exchange process.

In the bitcoin exchanges, the users who hold bitcoins enter in an 'ask price' i.e. the minimum price at which they are willing to part with their bitcoins. Any user who wants to buy the bitcoins enter in a 'bid price' i.e. the maximum price he is willing to pay to acquire bitcoins. When the bid price matches the ask price, the transaction is finalized and bitcoins flow from one party to the other.

Payment for Goods and Services

Bitcoins can also be accepted as a payment for goods sold and services rendered. Although bitcoin acceptance is not very high at the moment, the number of merchants accepting the payments has been increasing day after day.

Small merchants usually use a combination of accepting bitcoin payments along with other modes of payments. Bitcoin payments are processed faster, are secure and translate to lower fees for the merchant. Setting up bitcoin payments is a straightforward process.

Step 1: Choose a payment service.

There are multiple platforms that will let you add bitcoin acceptance capability to your business.

App based solutions - There are mobile application based solutions like Coin box[10] and Bitcoin Wallet App[11] which let merchants accept bitcoins. Merchants enter the price of the good or service which is generated as a QR code. This QR code is communicated to the buyer

---

10   play.google.com/store/apps/details?id=com.coinbox&hl=en_GB
11   play.google.com/store/apps/details?id=de.schildbach.wallet

who transfers the amount to merchant's bitcoin address. These solutions are ideal for small merchants with a limited number of transactions.

Point of Sale solutions - These are solutions for merchants who want a full-fledged platform solution for accepting bitcoins, for a large number of transactions or transactions of large value. Some of the recommended solutions are:

- Coinify - Coininfy (https://www.coinify.com/) arose from the merger of two firms BIPS and Coinzone. Coinify lets both the online as well as offline businesses accept bitcoins for their products. It also let the merchants withdraw funds to their account in fiat currency.

- Bit Pay - Bit Pay (https://bitpay.com/) is one of the most famous bitcoin point of sale solutions. Bit Pay offers a suite of additional extension like export to QuickBooks accounting software and also offers multiple subscription levels depending on the needs of the user.

- Coinbase - Coinbase (https://www.coinbase.com/merchants) is another very popular solution that serves merchants only in the USA. One of the key features of Coinbase solution is the readily available custom plugins for WordPress, WooCommerce, Shopify and ZenCart. It also provides a free service for processing the first USD 1 million in transactions.

Step 2: Connect your bank account and bitcoin address.

The next step is to connect your bank account and bitcoin wallet to the solution. You can connect your MasterCard/Visa or your bank account to withdraw funds to. At this step, you can also choose to enable other extensions. Once this step is complete, you can start accepting bitcoins.

If you anticipate that only a few transactions will occur in bitcoins, you can also choose to display a small banner stating 'bitcoins accepted' at a prominent place in your shop or online store. Buyers who wish to use this mode of payment can directly transfer the amount to your bitcoin address. This can help you start the process of accepting bitcoins and doesn't require any special solution or application.

Pricing of Bitcoins

Bitcoins are decentralized, which means the price of bitcoins is not set by any central authority but by the market mechanics of demand and supply. Because the supply of bitcoin is limited, a higher demand leads to an increase in the price of bitcoins.

The supply of bitcoins is constant and "...new bitcoins are created at a predictable and decreasing rate, which means that demand must follow this level of inflation to keep the price stable."[12]

Because of the low number of units in circulation, the price of bitcoin is very volatile. To date, the price of bitcoins has ranged from less than USD 0.01 to USD 1216.

Storage of Bitcoins - Different Wallets and Their Uses

The bitcoins that you own are stored in bitcoin wallets. You receive new bitcoins in your wallet as well. Earlier we talked about the safety of bitcoin transactions as opposed to other transactions online. This safety is highly dependent on the kind of wallet you choose to hold your bitcoins. One important thing to note here is the fact that bitcoin wallets, just like your normal wallets, are prone to dangers and must be secured properly.

Constituents of Wallets

Each bitcoin wallet contains two keys - a public key and a private key. These keys are used together to make transactions.

<u>Public Key</u>

A public key is a key which is accessible to everyone. This key is the address that other people send the bitcoins to.

---

12   https://bitcoin.org/en/faq#what-determines-bitcoins-price

Private Key

A private key is a key which is accessible only to you. It is the more important key of the two and is used to authorize the transaction along with the public key. If somebody gets his eyes on this key, he can use it to authorize transactions and withdraw your bitcoins.

Each bitcoin wallet contains a single or multiple private keys.

A private key associated with the transaction expires as soon as the transaction takes place and bitcoins are transferred. In some cases, the same key can be used again but this can compromise the security. A private key should preferably be used once only.

Kinds of Wallets

Just like there are different ways to store fiat currency like bank accounts, cash, credit card, there are different kinds of 'wallets' to store bitcoins.

There are four major kinds of wallets:

- Software Wallets
- Web Wallets
- Mobile Wallets
- Paper Wallets
- Hardware Wallets

These wallets are not exclusive to each other and bitcoins can be transferred from one wallet to another, just like fiat currency. Each kind of wallet has its own strengths and weaknesses. No wallet is inherently better than the other. Therefore, a lot of bitcoin users store their cryptocurrency in more than one wallet, at a time.

Software Wallets

Software Wallets are the most popular way of storing bitcoins. A software wallet is stored on your computer and gives you the most flexibility and control on your transactions.

Because a software wallet is stored on the computer, it is a very insecure wallet and is riddled with risks. The computer may be hacked and the wallet will be accessible to the hackers. The computer may die one day and along with the computer, the wallet and the bitcoins in that wallet will be lost forever.

> *Having a Software Wallet is akin to keeping your dollars in your pocket.*

It is not a good idea to store a large amount of bitcoins on a software wallet because of the obvious risks. A small amount, however, can be kept safely if some safety measures are followed.

The first step after getting a software wallet should be to encrypt the wallet so that it is not *as easily accessible* to the hackers. Most of the software wallets come with encryption software. After encryption, you will be prompted for a password every time you open your software wallet. This will help secure your wallet, but only to some extent. The wallet can still be easily hacked by installing software to hack your password.

The second step should be to back up your wallet. Just like you back up photos and documents to retrieve them in case of a crash or a hack, it is a good idea to back up your software wallet. You can use any one of the two commonly used ways of backing up the files - external hard drive and online backup. Hard drives can be lost and online backups can be hacked into. You can also use pre-internet encryption (using an encryption method before backing up files to the internet) to back up your software wallet. This method is safer than other methods.

Again, these are ways to improve the security of your software wallet but they don't eliminate the risks completely.

Creating a software wallet isn't a complicated process.

Step 1: Choose a software wallet.

There are a variety of software wallets to choose from. Some of the most recommended software wallets are:

- Electrum - Electrum (https://electrum.org) is encrypted by default, making it secure. The installation process is simple and easy to follow. After the installation finishes, you are given a twelve word phrase which you can use to recover your bitcoins if you lose your wallet. It also verifies all the transactions in your wallet occasionally.

- Bitcoin Core - Bitcoin Core (https://bitcoin.org/en/download), formerly Bitcoin QT, is the most secure software wallet and runs on the bitcoin protocol. However, the security comes at a cost. The wallet hogs up upload bandwidth and has often been criticized as slow at syncing the transactions after they are confirmed.

- Multibit - Multibit (https://multibit.org) is a 'lightweight' and slightly improved version of Bitcoin Core. A multibit wallet supports multiple languages and multiple wallets. Multibit is faster and doesn't download the entire blockchain information on the computer. It also allows the user to import and export wallet keys.

Apart from these famous software wallet clients, power users like using Armory which has better encryption software and is more secure overall.

Step 2: Secure your wallet

Securing the wallet means encrypting it using a software, setting up the password for day-to-day usage and finally backing it up - both on a hard drive and an online server after pre-internet encrypting. You should back up your wallet after regular intervals of time.

Services like Dropbox are not recommended because they let your data be available to their employees and other personnel with access. It is vital to choose a good service to back up the data.

Some services like Multibit also give you the option of creating 'wallet words'. This is essentially a safe-word that can be used to access your account in a special event. The safe-word is different from the password which will be used every time you open your wallet.

Step 3: Creation of multiple wallets

After securing the wallet, you are free to create multiple wallets and do as many transactions as you wish.

Web Wallets

As the name suggests, web wallets are wallets that are operated over the web. Although these are the most convenient kind of wallets, yet they are the riskiest. Your coins are hosted on an online server, any event of hacking the website or likewise can result in lost bitcoins.

Having a Web Wallet is akin to keeping your dollars in a bank account.

One of the former largest bitcoin exchanges which handled almost 80% of bitcoin transactions at a time, Mt. Gox was also used as a web wallet by many. It was hacked a number of times, resulting in many displaced bitcoins. The company lost 650000 bitcoins[13] to hackers in its lifetime and was declared bankrupt in 2014.

Although an online server hosts your bitcoins, it doesn't guarantee a risk free store of value which the commercial banks do. This is one of the reasons why a bulk of users opt to keep majority of their bitcoins in either software or paper wallets.

What they lack in security, they make up for it in convenience. Web wallets make it extremely simple for a novice to conduct transactions and store bitcoins. Lacking in security now, it is expected that the web wallets will grow to be more secure with the increasing advancements in the Bitcoin protocol as well as the technology.

Like a software wallet, signing up for a web wallet is simple.

Step 1: Choose a web wallet.

There are tens of organizations that offer web wallet services. Because of security issues, it is prudent to select one which suits your needs. Some of the most popular bitcoin web wallets are:

---

13 http://www.bbc.com/news/technology-26677291

- My Wallet by Blockchain-My Wallet (https://blockchain.info/wallet/) is one of the most popular and user-friendly wallets which boast zero fees. Blockchain wallets take care of security by enabling encryption activity within the browser before uploading to Blockchain servers, protecting the details of account even from it. It becomes important to update your browser extensions regularly.

- Coinbase Wallet - Coinbase (https://www.coinbase.com/) offers a user-friendly wallet along with a mobile app and provides capability to merchants to accept payments. One of the striking features of a Coinbase wallet is the fact that they insure the bitcoins in your account. They also promise the security by establishing and using offline servers to hold bitcoins. Moreover, they provide you the option of scheduling bitcoin buying or selling transactions.

- Copay Wallet - Copay Wallet (https://copay.io/) is a relatively new entrant in the web wallet arena. A wallet that offers an option to create an actual 'wallet', it allows multiple users to hold one account. It also supports a full bitcoin payment protocol encryption rewarding security to its users.

- BitGo Wallet - BitGo Wallet (https://www.bitgo.com/wallet) handles personal as well as business wallets. The wallet offers you the capability to log in various users. BitGo also allows you to set controls monitoring the bitcoins usage. It also provides for instant alerts and two-step verification to take care of security concerns.

Step 2: Secure your wallet.

The next step is to create a wallet. After creating the wallet, you will be given an option to secure your wallet by setting up a phrase or a safe-word in case of any incident. You will be given a phase and a recovery sheet to note down the safe-word generated by the web wallet.

Mobile Wallets

Mobile wallets are usually an added feature of various web wallets, which provide a mobile application in order to facilitate transactions along with the browser-based wallet. The basic purpose of a mobile wallet is to enable you to perform the operations from a mobile in place of a browser.

Some mobile wallets however are mobile-only. One of the most popular and the first mobile wallet is called Bitcoin Wallet.

Bitcoin Wallet[14], a peer-to-peer decentralized wallet, offers many features to its users, including but not limited to, a QR based method in addition to a NFC and a URL based method of facilitating transactions, quick conversion to and from local currencies, an address book, sweeping of paper wallets and a mechanism to pay when offline.

Clearly it is one of the most secure and recommended methods of holding bitcoins. Starting with Bitcoin Wallet is a two-step process - downloading the application on the mobile phone and using it to buy/sell/trade bitcoins. Even a registration is not required.

Another notable mention here is Paytunia by Paymium. Paytunia is a mobile wallet for the browser based wallet by Paymium. Paymium is also an exchange in addition to a wallet.

Paper Wallets

Paper wallet is one which allows you to keep your bitcoins *independent* of a computer. It is an offline storage wallet. This is the most secure way of keeping bitcoins because paper wallets cannot be decrypted or hacked. Paper wallet is similar to keeping cash in your pocket.

> *Having a Paper Wallet is like*
> *keeping your dollars in a safe deposit box.*

Before going further, it is important to understand that the risk to bitcoins is a risk of private key being lost or accessed by hackers. In

---

14   Access at https://play.google.com/store/apps/details?id=de.schildbach.wallet&hl=en

all other kinds of wallets, the private key is stored online, either on the computer or over the web. The paper wallet is based on the idea that if private key is stored offline, it will be *almost* impossible to hack into.

The keys for a paper wallet are generated offline and stored on a paper which never sees the internet. Storing a digital currency in paper form may seem odd, but is still the securest wallet amongst the options. However, paper is a fragile object and the ink used to print can easily degrade. Therefore, extreme caution must be exercised while using paper wallets.

A paper wallet contains the public key and the private keys as well the QR codes for quick scanning.

The process for setting up a paper wallet is not complicated. You can either use Bitcoin Address or Blockchain to accomplish this.

Step 1: Creating a Bitcoin Wallet Using Bitcoin Address

Method 1 - In your browser, go to https://www.bitaddress.org/ to create a new bitcoin address. Once the website loads, you will be asked to randomly move your mouse or type some alphabets. After the completion of this step, a public and private key along with the QR codes will be generated.

Go to the 'Paper Wallet' tab, where you will be given an option to remove the art and input the number of addresses to generate. After selecting the options, click on 'Generate' to generate wallet as per your specifications.

Once the wallet is generated, print the wallet by using Ctrl + P. You may also save the wallet as a PDF file on your computer. The paper wallet has now been created, you can scan the public key to your mobile app and use the public address to load your wallet with bitcoins.

Method 2 - In your browser, go to https://www.bitaddress.org/ to create a new bitcoin address. Once the website loads, use Ctrl + S in a PC, or Command + S in a Mac to save the website as an HTML file.

Switch off the internet, save this file to a USB Device and switch off your computer. Restart your computer with a bootable Linux Live CD.

The CD will ensure that the computer is safe and the internet is off. This step, although not necessary, can bring an added layer of security to the transaction.

Click on the file that you saved and open it in a browser, without connecting back to the internet. Now you will see the website loading without the internet on. From here on, follow the same instructions as above.

The paper wallet you created using the second method is the safest option to create and use a wallet because it was never online and didn't give anybody opportunity to lay eyes on it.

Step 2: Using Bitcoin Paper Wallet through Blockchain

After the generation of the public and private keys, you would need an application to carry out the transactions. Blockchain mobile application can be used for the process. After downloading the app, you will be asked to scan your public key with a 'Watch Only' access.

Once the address is entered in the app, you can use the address to transfer bitcoins to the wallet or watch the balance of funds. You can also use the app to send coins. To do this, you will be asked to scan your private key in order to authorize the transaction.

A paper wallet can be redeemed and used to pay for transactions, at any point in time, by using exchanges.

Hardware Wallets

Hardware wallets are an improvement over software wallets and paper wallets. Hardware wallets cannot be hacked by computer viruses. Unlike software wallets, the private key in hardware wallets is stored in the microcontroller, a protected area, and hence free from the risk of transfer. Unlike paper wallets, hardware wallets can work independently and do not need to be imported back to be used.

Managing Security Concerns

- Don't use a shared computer to access wallets or a shared printer to print paper wallets.

- Make the wallet creation process private. Don't let anybody see your private key(s) while the wallet is being generated.

- Store your paper wallet in a sealed plastic bag or get it laminated. This will help you ensure safety of your paper wallet.

- Use a private key only once.

Choosing the Right Wallet

All wallets have their pros and cons, strengths and weaknesses. It is important to choose the wallet which is right for your needs. It is recommended to use multiple kinds of wallets to enable a smooth transaction experience in all contexts.

- Choose a paper wallet for long-term investments in bitcoins. Paper wallets are the most secure form of wallets and can easily be kept safe without noticeable intervention for a large period of time.

- Choose a web wallet to keep small amounts of bitcoins for day-to-day usage. This will help you process the transactions in the least possible time conveniently. A mobile wallet, usually an extension of the web wallet, will help you facilitate the same transactions with ease through an app in your mobile phone.

- Choose a hardware wallet to keep a relatively larger number of bitcoins for miscellaneous usage. They will keep the currency safe and allow for relatively quicker transactions if and when the need arises.

- Choose a paper wallet if you want to give bitcoins as gifts or tokens of appreciation as it will make it easier for you to handle the transaction.

Transferring Bitcoins between Wallets

Exchanges can be used to transfer funds from one kind of wallet to another. Just visit the exchange's website, log in and select the option 'Withdraw Funds' from the trading tab. Once this step is successfully completed, you will be prompted to put in the amount and the address of the Bitcoin account. This will permanently and irreversibly transfer the bitcoins from your old wallet to your new wallet.

Bitcoin ATMs

As we talked in Chapter 2, bitcoin ATMs are a relatively new feature. Bitcoin ATMs started in 2013 when Robocoin launched the first Bitcoin kiosk in Vancouver, Canada. The kiosk was a huge success, in part, because the coffee shop outside which it was opened accepted bitcoins as a form of payment. Robocoin started a revolution and soon other players entered the market and took over. Robocoin is not a major player in the market anymore.

There are 669 Bitcoin ATMs spread over 16 countries but primarily concentrated in the USA, Canada and Europe. The US alone accounts for 325 of these 669 Bitcoin ATMs. 224 of the total 369 ATMs are operated by Genesis Coin.

The bitcoin ATMs have lent an aura of authenticity to the Bitcoin economy. Bitcoin ATMs can help you buy and sell bitcoins.

Buy Bitcoins

Buying bitcoins through a Bitcoin ATM is a simple process. When you visit an ATM machine, you will be asked to verify yourself. This is an optional step. The next step is to enter in your Bitcoin address enabling the machine to transfer bitcoins to that address. Some ATMs give you the option of creating an address as well. Then, you put in the requisite amount of cash to carry out the operation. The last step is to confirm that the transaction has taken place.

After you have put in the cash, you can either take a receipt of your private key from the kiosk or you can have the key sent to your email protected by a password that you input. You can also send the bitcoins to the bitcoin address that you entered earlier. Some ATM operators even give you the option of sending in the bitcoins to your hardware wallet.

The exact procedure varies at ATMs handled by different operators.

Sell Bitcoins

The procedure to sell a bitcoin also requires verification as the first step. The next step is to send the amount of bitcoins you want to sell to address, usually displayed as a QR code. After you dial in the entry, you will be able to withdraw the cash out of the machine. Some machines do not let you withdraw cash, but they give you a redeem code which you can use after the confirmations go through.

Things to Remember While Using an ATM

1) Not every ATM allows you to sell bitcoins. There are one-way (buy only) and two-way ATMs. Two-way ATMs are about 40% of all Bitcoin ATMs. Determine the kind of ATM before you make the trip.

2) Before going to an ATM, do your research. Find out if it's a one-way or a two-way ATM. Also find out the operator of the ATM machine and understand how the particular model works.

3) You can use https://coinatmradar.com/ or http://www.coindesk.com/bitcoin-atm-map/ to find the nearest ATM from your location. You can also search for ATMs selling other cryptocurrencies.

4) Bitcoin ATMs have made buying and selling bitcoins an easy process. But you still need to be careful around the receipts that you print from these ATMs. These receipts sometimes carry public as well as private key of the owner.

Quick Recap

This section has become a little technical. Therefore, a quick summary elucidating the main points is included.

- There are four major ways to acquire bitcoins.
    - **Mining** - Mining is the only way to generate new bitcoins in the system. It works like mining of physical gold.

- **Over The Counter Exchanges** - OTC Exchange is exchange of bitcoins in a physical location, just like you would exchange money in person when you buy a real estate asset.

- **Bitcoin Exchanges** - Bitcoin exchanges are similar to the stock exchanges and facilitate buying and selling of bitcoins.

- **Payment for Goods and Services** - Bitcoins can also be acquired by selling your goods or services in exchange for bitcoins.

* Bitcoins are priced on the basis of market dynamics of demand and supply. This ensures that the inflation doesn't diminish the value of the currency.

* Once you acquire bitcoins, they will need to be stored somewhere. Just like you store your dollars in your wallet and bank account, you can store bitcoins in wallets.

* Each wallet contains a public key and a private key to facilitate transactions. Public key is the address which is visible to everyone whereas the private key is the key which acts as an authorization mechanism (akin to a signature) to approve payments.

* There are four major kinds of wallets, each with its own security along with other strengths and weaknesses.

    - **Software Wallet** - Software wallets are stored on your computer. They are the easiest to use but pose considerable security risks.

    - **Web Wallet** - Web wallets are operated over the web. They are flexible in nature but most susceptible to fraud and hacking.

    - **Mobile Wallet** - Mobile wallets are usually just an extension of web wallets on mobile. They carry the same risks as web wallets.

    - **Paper Wallet** - Paper wallets are offline storage wallets and allow you to keep your bitcoins independent of a computer. They are the most secure way of keeping bitcoins but very inflexible and tiresome to use for everyday transactions.

- A new kind of wallet, **hardware wallets**, is an improvement over software wallets and paper wallets. Unlike software wallets, Hardware wallets cannot be hacked by computer viruses. Unlike paper wallets, hardware wallets can work independently and do not need to be imported back to be used.

- Every wallet is fit for different occasions. A person should ideally keep his bitcoins in two or more wallets. For example - a paper wallet should be used for long-term investments and web wallet for daily transactions.

- Just like bank ATMs, there are Bitcoin ATMs which allow you to buy and sell bitcoins at convenience. This has greatly increased the legitimacy of bitcoins.

Chapter 4 - Bitcoin Transaction Process

Bitcoins transactions are secure, painless and straightforward transactions. In this chapter, we will discuss the process flow of a bitcoin transaction and how mining works in detail.

The Problem of Double Spending

When you give your friend a USD $100 bill, you no longer have it. With the physical exchange of the bill, you have also transferred the value associated with the money to your friend and can no longer use it. This is true for all physical goods, including documents and money.

When we come to their digital counterparts, we start seeing problems. When you send a PDF document or even an email to your friend, you still have a copy of it. The copy is usable - you can make changes to the documents and refer to it for other purposes. Your friend can do the same. He can make copies of the document that he received while retaining one with himself. Theoretically, each document can be made into infinite copies without causing any deterioration in value to the original document. In fact, each document is as good as the original.

This is highly convenient for documents but disastrous for bitcoins.

What if you transfer 10 BTC (10 bitcoins) to your friend but still retain them? This will lead to the generation of infinite copies of those bitcoins. Because of infinite copies, each particular unit will now become worthless.[15*]

---

15 * For a currency to be valuable, it needs to be scarce. Let us say, you have 100 one dollar notes and only a finite number of notes are in supply in the economy. You decide to get a haircut for yourself by using 5 of the 100 bills. You part with the money in exchange for the service and the hairdresser earns money for providing the service.

To avoid the problem of duplicity, the bitcoin network requires the use of a regulator or an intermediary who can keep a record of the bitcoins transactions in order to match funds to the rightful owner.

To understand the role of an intermediary, let us imagine a transaction when X is paying USD $100 to Y (who has an account in Bank Q) using his Visa debit card issued by Bank P. X swipes the card or enters in the details at the gateway provided by Y. This information is recorded by Visa as well as Bank P. After Visa and Bank P match their records, Bank P debits X's account by USD 100. Visa communicates this to Bank Q who then credits Y's account by USD 100. The intermediaries help record as well as verify the transaction.

Because bitcoin is a decentralized peer-to-peer service, there are no central authorities or regulators. Instead bitcoin uses a system called 'blockchain', which relies on users to keep track of transactions and prevent fraudulent activities at the same time.

A Sample Bitcoin Transaction

Let us understand the process of transfer of bitcoins from one user to another through a transaction between A and B.

A has purchased a book from B and wants to pay him using bitcoins. Let us assume that B is a book seller who has a heavyweight point-of-sale solution for accepting bitcoins. B enters USD 50, the price of the book in the system which displays it in both USD and BTC terms for the convenience of the customer.

After a nod from A, he is shown the QR code at which he should transfer the money. A uses his mobile application to scan the QR code which

---

> Now let us say that the government passes a law allowing you to print currency at home. You become very happy and immediately print 100 more one dollar notes. Now instead of going to the same hairdresser, you decide to go to a better one. You visit the hairdresser but he refuses to provide you any service. He tells you that he doesn't need to work now, he can just print however much money he wants. In other words, money is valuable only because it's scarce.
>
> This trend will continue and in a very short time, money will become valueless. And we will look for another medium of exchange which is finite in nature and valuable to the service provider.

populates the sender's address and the amount in his application. He uses his digital signature to validate the transaction and the amount is transferred to B's bitcoin wallet.

Nuances of the Transaction

Whenever you receive bitcoins, you store them in your wallet without any change. For example, before doing the above transaction, A purchased 2 BTC from the Bitcoin Exchange and got 3 BTC as a gift from his friend F. The BTC will be stored as-it-is in his wallet without any addition or sum up. In other words, instead of having a single balance of 5 BTC, A will have a transaction for 2 BTC and another one for 3 BTC in his account.

If A has to transfer 1 BTC to B for B's services, he cannot divide the first transaction into 2 parts of 1 BTC each because, as a rule, each input has to be fully consumed in the process of exchange. Instead he will have to send the entire 2 BTC to B (the combination of transactions to be sent is usually calculated by the application), who will then return 1 BTC back to A. This will be processed as two entries in the same transaction.

When A had received BTC from various sources, a copy of that transaction was entered into the network. The copy will be maintained in the system forever.

Now, let us rewind a bit to understand the mechanics of the transaction. Each transaction has three components:

- Input - Input is the reference to transactions from which the bitcoins are transferred. In our example, these are the reference codes of the transactions through which A received BTC.
- Amount - This is the amount of the bitcoins that is being transferred. In our example, it is BTC equivalent to USD 50.
- Output - Output is the address to which the bitcoins are being transferred. In our example, it is B's public address.[16*]

---
16 *Apart from this, there can be other cases like an input being distributed into multiple outputs such as payment of wages or multiple inputs being merged into one output.

For the avoidance of double spending, this transaction must be recorded somewhere and the accounts must be updated simultaneously. When A transfers agreed on amount of bitcoins to B, two processes are taking place simultaneously - the authentication of the transfer (verification of the change in ownership) plus recording and approval of the transfer (establishment of change in ownership).

When A sends a request to the network consisting of the input, amount and output, the inputs are cross-referenced with the existing records of transactions in the Bitcoin network. Once the inputs are confirmed to exist and unused, the next step is to check the validity of transaction. When A sends the message, there is no way to confirm if the request was actually generated by A or someone else entirely. Therefore, A needs to send a 'signed' request to the bitcoin network, proving he was indeed the initiator of the transaction.

To authenticate the transaction message, A will have to use his private key. The private key acts like a signature corroborating the truthfulness of the transaction. The digital signature is created by using a combination of the private key and the message (consisting of the input, amount and output). A mathematical function automatically generates the signature for A.

After the request is transmitted, a different mathematical function checks the signature to verify if the signature matches A's request. Here the network is able to confirm that A owned the private key and is authorized to carry out the transaction, without even seeing the private key, thereby maintaining the security.[17+]

Once verification of A's identity and the message is completed, the bitcoin network records and approves this request using 'blockchain' and the amount is transferred, which is reflected in the funds balance on A's and B's account.

---

17 + Because the signature consists of both the private key and the message which is unique to each transaction, the signature cannot be used again. Because message is an important part of the signature, no one can change the nature of the transaction while recording and approving it.

In fact, any such attempt would invalidate the signature and nullify the transaction.

Blockchain

Blockchain is essentially a public ledger which holds entries of all bitcoin transactions. This is a global ledger which is decentralized and operated by volunteers across the globe.

When A transfers BTC to B, the transaction is recorded in the public ledger. Now let us say, A immediately goes to another shop and buys a service worth 10 BTC from C. The same payment process will follow and the entry will be added after A's previous transaction entry into the blockchain. A's previous entry will, in fact, be used as a secure record for verification of A's new entry.

A blockchain can be visualized as a vertical pile of entries stacked over one another in order to create a block. Because this block of transactions is available to everybody across the system and each new block is added to the collective blocks before it, it acts as a chain that connects all nodes.

Each block contains records of transactions that happened during a particular period of time. Depending on the number of people who are recording and approving the transactions, the time of each block keeps on changing but usually stays around the mark of 10 minutes. Continuing the above example, A's funds will actually be transferred to B after the block is entered into the chain i.e. after ten minutes.

The blockchain, which is distributed globally, has a record of all transactions that have ever taken place using bitcoins.

Miners and Mining

The group of volunteers who enable blockchain process are called miners and the activity of generating new bitcoins using the processing power of computing and hardware is called mining.

The miners essentially perform two functions for each block

1) Recording of transactions
2) Approval of transactions

Whenever the input, amount and output are broadcasted, the broadcast is made to the entire group of miners. Each miner uses his computational and hardware capabilities to record the transactions that take place within a particular duration of time. Each such record of entries, called a block is created and then added to the previous block completing the chain. A copy of this blockchain is provided to each miner across the network.

All of the information regarding the transactions, held in blockchain, is stored in the cloud. Anything which is held digitally comes with risk of being hacked, broken into or tampered with. If the blockchain is susceptible to such frauds, bitcoins will not be secure and therefore, lose some of the legitimacy that they have gained. Therefore, the information in each block goes through the process of encryption before it is added to all the blocks preceding it and stored online.

The encryption technique used here is called hashing. A hash is a function which changes the transaction message into a series of random unrelated numbers. Because the numbers are random, the hash is a one-way function which means that the hash cannot be converted back into the original transaction message. The hash, therefore, hides information about the block and adds to the security of the Bitcoin network.

Each transaction in a block has a hash associated with it. These hashes combine to create a block hash which is added into the block along with the transactions. When a new block is created, it starts with the hash of the previous block in its header. This ensures that the block is connected to the right block i.e. the block immediately preceding it. This also makes sure that a timeline with respect to the transactions is established. Whenever the block is formed, the transactions are deemed to be approved.

Each block is connected to the previous block by hash. In fact, a block is formed only when the hash is created. Since hash is a one-way function, it is almost impossible to go back to the transactions using the hash. This increases the security of the system.[18+]

---

18 +The process of blockchain coupled with the principles of cryptography result in a highly secure network. Because a copy of blockchain is available to all miners

Chapter 4: Bitcoin Transaction Process

For miners, creating a hash for the block of transactions is the 'Proof of Work' and this is what they get rewarded bitcoins for. When a transaction is broadcasted to the network, all miners start trying to generate the hash for the block. The hash is based on the transactions in the block, the hash of previous block and possesses the mathematical property of being less than a number known as target value.

The only way for miners to find the right hash is to try all possible scenarios. This process requires time, memory and computing power. The miner who cracks it the first broadcasts it to the entire network and earns a reward in form of bitcoins for the same. Because solving the problem requires checking of a variety of permutations and combinations every time, the process is random to an extent and provides a level playing field for all miners.

As soon as one block is confirmed, miners start working on the next block of transactions and the process continues.

The average time it takes for one block to be processed is 10 minutes. When more miners join the network, the block creation process fastens and the average time it takes to mine one block decreases. Because of the fall in average time, mining becomes a substantially more difficult activity. This results in fall in the block creation rate and subsequently the average time per block. Therefore, the automatic correction mechanism takes care of the average time it takes to mine a block. As a result, the mining time remains almost constant at 10 minutes.

The process is referred to as mining because the number of bitcoins that the miners receive from processing transactions decreases over time[19*], similar to mining of metals and precious elements.

---

    across the network, it is difficult to tamper with it. Any change in one node will create a discrepancy within the whole network. This makes bitcoins very secure to work with.

19 * The amount of bitcoins halves every 210000 blocks which roughly translates to 4 years. During the first four years, miners received a reward of 50 BTC per block, this was reduced to 25 BTC in 2012 and is set to further reduce to 12.5 BTC this year.

45

Pooling

In the previous section, we discussed how the difficulty of mining increases as more and more people join the network. Because of the increasing difficulty, the time it takes to mine one block increases.

At the current difficulty level of 209,453,158,595 it would take a solo miner *years* to mine one block.[20]

The process of mining would be highly infeasible if it took a miner years to mine one block. The payoff is very uncertain and too far ahead in the future to be comforting or even compelling enough to motivate the miner to continue. This may even lead to a decrease in the number of miners and reduce the tight security of the Bitcoin network.

To combat this problem and allow smaller miners to be competent and stay in the market, miners join to form a group to do mining collectively.

This group is called a pool. In a pool, different miners with varying processing capabilities join hands to mine a block together and share the mining rewards (i.e. the bitcoins generated) in proportion to their contribution to the pool in terms of the processing capability.

Going Solo or Pooling

One of the biggest questions while starting with mining is the decision to mine alone or go with a pool. There is no best approach to this problem. Both the approaches have their advantages and limitations.

One thing to understand before taking the decision is that both approaches inherently carry the same risk-and-reward combinations. Going solo allows you a greater reward but it will take you longer to mine a block whereas pooling will make it faster to mine a block but the reward will be shared and hence lower.

With the current standing of bitcoins, it is extremely difficult for a solo miner to make money by himself because of the increased mining

---

20 https://bitcoinwisdom.com/bitcoin/difficulty

difficulty. It would be useful for him, therefore, to join a pool. Pooling would give him easier access as well as quicker returns.

The decision to go with either one of them should be motivated by your preference for the nature and time of reward along with your willingness to invest in mining equipment. If you are willing to wait for a higher reward and have the desire and willingness to invest in bulk of equipment, go solo. Otherwise, it is better to join a pool.

Getting Started With Mining

Miners are rewarded with bitcoins for processing the transactions (which is how new bitcoins are generated in the system) and also get bitcoins as transaction fees. As the amount of BTC released through mining decreases with time, the transaction fees will increase to compensate the miners. The miners shouldn't be worried about the decreasing amount of bitcoins after certain blocks.

The procedure for getting started with mining is straightforward.

Step 1: Select mining equipment.

The first step while deciding to go for mining is to decide on the mining equipment. During the first year after the bitcoins were started, it was easy enough to mine them using your personal computer's processing powers. But that's no longer possible. Because of the high number of miners in the market, you now need to purchase professional mining equipment.

Because mining cannot be performed with your regular run of the mill computers, you need a special kind of computer with a simplified motherboard, an extraordinary cooling facilities and GPU cards for provision of processing capabilities. You can buy dedicated hardware and make your own rig. However this causes a lot of overheating in the premises where you house them and the entire operation may consume more in electricity than you can make using mining.

Therefore, new kinds of hardware were developed specifically for the purpose of mining. They include custom made chips for bitcoin mining. With a specified hash rate and significantly lower power consumption, they make for a better equipment for dedicated mining.

The most important thing while buying any equipment is the hash rate. The hash rate is the rate at which your hardware can perform mathematical calculations which enable mining. The higher the hash rate, the faster the mining process.

Some of the most recommended equipment for mining is:

- **AntMiner S7** - With one of the highest capacity amongst the equipment at 4.73 Th/s, the AntMiner S7 is also one of the most energy efficient and uses only 0.25 W/Gh. It weighs a little less than 9 pounds and is priced around USD 600.

The AntMiner S7 can earn approximately 0.4 bitcoins a month.

- **Avalon6** - One of the pricier options in the market at USD 750, Avalon6 has a capacity of around 3.5 Th/s. This is coupled with a 0.29 W/Gh power efficiency. This is a slightly heavier machine at around 10 pounds.

The Avalon6can earn approximately 0.3 bitcoins a month.

- **SP20 Jackson** - With a weight of 20 pounds and capacity of only 1.5 Th/s, this may seem like an under par equipment. But it is one of the cheapest in the market at nearly USD 250.

The SP20 Jackson can earn approximately 0.15 bitcoins a month.

As we discussed earlier, the choice of machine should take into consideration the processing capacity as well as the cost. One thing which should also be taken into consideration is the power requirements and the consequent electricity costs, lest they turn the entire gig unprofitable.

Cloud Mining

Instead of buying hardware, you can also choose to opt for cloud mining. As the name suggests, cloud mining involves use of equipment hosted online instead of physical hardware. Cloud mining is not very popular with professional miners because it isn't very secure. In the past, there have been a number of instances of hacks into various cloud mining operations.

There are a number of reasons that people, usually beginners, go for cloud mining. With cloud mining, they get the option of starting with a minimal of constraints. There is no need to buy expensive equipment, deal with exorbitant electricity bills or install cooling machines all over the place.

All of this, however, comes at the cost of a significantly reduced profit.

Cloud mining requires the use of your normal computer, which is used to control and manage the mining happening over the web. Cloud Mining is generally used in three ways:

- **Hosted Mining**- Hosted mining involves leasing of a machine such as the AntMiner S7 which is hosted by the service provider.

- **Virtual Hosted Mining**- Virtual hosted mining includes setting up a new virtual private server and then installation of the mining software.

- **Leased Hashing Power**- As the name suggests, leased hashing power is leasing of hashing power, instead of leasing a machine or setting up a remote server. There is no need to maintain a dedicated physical or virtual computer for mining using this method.

Leased Hashing Power is one of the most popular ways of using cloud mining.

There are costs involved in the process of cloud mining. You need to pay your service provider a monthly charge or cost in relation to the processing power bought. Consequently, the plans may start from as low as USD 10 per month.

Some of the most widely used cloud mining services[21*] are the following:

- Hashflare
- Genesis Mining
- Hashner
- Minergate
- Hashnest
- Nicehash
- Bitcoin Cloud Mining
- Eobot
- Mine on cloud

Be careful while choosing from amongst the two options - owning your hardware and cloud mining.

Step 2: Select a mining software.

The next step after purchase of hardware is to install a mining software. The bitcoin mining software connects you to the blockchain. If you are a solo miner, it is a good idea to use the official Bitcore client[22] as it will ensure that you are in a consensus with the Bitcoin network.

Otherwise, you can also select from the following mining software:

- **For Windows** – Mine Peon, Easy Miner, Bit Moose
- **For Mac OSX** – Mine Peon, Diablo Miner
- **ASIC** – BFG Miner, CG Miner[23+]
- **Cloud Mining software** – Hashflare, Genesis Mining

---

21 * The cloud mining services discussed are the ones which are widely used. However because of the services being susceptible to hacking, they are not recommended at all. Do not consider this a list of the best or the most recommended services. Discretion advised.
22 Bitcoin Core can be accessed at https://bitcoin.org/en/download Please note that the download will take considerable time and space.
23 + These are also available for Windows and Mac OSX

Each software will fulfill different needs. Therefore, it is important to research every one of the available options and match the features against your needs in order to select the one which is a right fit.

Step 3: Start mining.

Once you have completed these two steps, you can start mining. Before you can do that, please ensure that you have a proper internet connection and appropriate coolers to regulate the heat generated, if you choose a physical equipment for the purpose of mining.

These steps apply to you as a solo miner. If you wish to pool, the steps will be somewhat different. The steps that apply to pooling are discussed below.

Getting Started With Pooling

Getting started with pooling is a little more tedious than getting started with mining. The steps will largely remain the same, but the decision to choose a pool can be tricky and prove to be a time consuming activity.

Step 1: Select a pool.

The first step would be to select a pool that matches your needs. Each pool has its own set of requirements. Go through the set of requirements before making a decision.

Some of the most famous mining pools are:

- **AntPool** - Situated in China, AntPool is the biggest mining pool currently. It controls a little more than a quarter of the Bitcoin network.

- **F2 Pool** - The second largest mining pool, F2 pool is also based out of China. It also controls almost a quarter of the network. Because of Chinese being a predominant language of instruction, this pool isn't preferred by non-native Chinese.

- **Other Pools** - There are various other pools out there, each controlling some part of the bitcoin network.

While choosing a pool, do keep in mind that different pools share rewards[24+] in different ways. Choose one that is in sync with your needs at the moment.

Step 2: Select the mining hardware and software.

While pooling, it is important to select the hardware equipment and software that is in line with the requirements of your pool. You must also ensure a fast and reliable internet connection at all times.

Quick Recap

This section has become a little technical. Therefore, a quick summary elucidating the main points is included.

- Using bitcoins is a very secure method of executing transactions. This is mainly because of the multiple levels of checks in-built into the system. The main checks are the following.
    - Each transaction request is matched to the ones previously carried out by the system. This ensures that all money is accounted for and no fraud is being perpetrated.
    - Each transaction is recorded in a public ledger which is open to everyone. Any discrepancy in any transaction at any node of the network is easily detected in the network.
    - Not only this, a group of transactions is recorded together in a block. All these blocks are connected to each another, making it further very difficult to breach the security.
- The people who maintain the public ledgers and handle blockchain are called miners. Miners get bitcoins as rewards for approving the transactions as valid and recording them by making and connecting blocks.

---

24 + There are pools who pay per share and guarantee an almost regular payout whereas there are others which pay according to target i.e. according to the difficulty of the problem solved by the miner.

These should influence your choice of a pool. You can read more about the various methods of reward sharing followed by different pools at https://en.wikipedia.org/wiki/Mining_pool#Mining_pool_methods

- Mining of bitcoins is similar to mining gold, the difference being the equipment used. You use your computer's processing power to mine bitcoins.

- Because of increase in the number of miners, mining difficulty has increased in the recent times. Therefore, a lot of miners find it more profitable to work together in a group and combine all their processing powers. This practice is referred to as pooling.

- Getting started with mining and pooling is a straightforward process and involves procurement of necessary hardware and installation of a software.

Chapter 5 - Selling and Trading Bitcoins

This brings us to the most important part of investing in bitcoins - trading or selling them in exchange for a neat profit. This chapter details the tools and techniques required to trading efficiently. It also covers the legal aspects of the sale and tax requirements, if any.

Trading and Selling Bitcoins

Just like there are various ways of acquiring bitcoins, there are various ways of selling them. The major ways are:

1) Bitcoin exchanges
2) Payment for goods and services
3) Over The Counter exchange

Bitcoin exchanges

Bitcoin exchanges are places where bitcoin users meet each other in order to sell or buy bitcoins. Bitcoin exchanges help you exchange bitcoins without meeting the other party.

The process of selling bitcoins using Bitcoin Exchanges is similar to the bitcoin buying process using the same exchanges and the steps remain the same. You select an exchange, connect your wallet and offer bitcoins for sale. (Please refer to the section on Bitcoin Exchanges in Chapter 3)

You can input your own ask price i.e. the price that you are willing to sell your bitcoins at. Although you can set the price at any range, you can guarantee a quick sale if the ask price is close to the market price.

Despite the security concerns, bitcoin exchanges remain a popular way to trade bitcoins.

Payment for goods and services

Bitcoins can also be given as a payment to the seller in exchange for goods or services. You can use a mobile wallet to ensure convenience, while the other methods work well too. (Please refer to the section on 'Payment for goods and services' in Chapter 3)

Not every business accepts bitcoins. The trick is to find out which ones do. You can use the following links to find out a list of businesses that do accept bitcoins.

- http://www.coindesk.com/information/what-can-you-buy-with-bitcoins/
- https://99bitcoins.com/who-accepts-bitcoins-payment-companies-stores-take-bitcoins/

You will be surprised to find out that many established businesses like Microsoft, Dell and WordPress and even some Non Profit Organizations accept bitcoins as a form of payment.

Over The Counter Exchange

As the name suggests, Over The Counter or OTC exchange is exchange of cash for bitcoins in a physical location. The users meet at a pre-decided location, where the buyer pays the seller the decided amount of cash and other requisite information for buying bitcoins.

The procedure for selling bitcoins is the exact same as the one for buying. (Please refer to the section on 'Over The Counter Exchanges' in Chapter 3)

Conversion Back Into Dollars

If you sell/trade your bitcoins using an OTC exchange, you can request the other party to transfer the money right into your account. On the other hand, while selling bitcoins using exchanges, you have two options. You can choose to keep the money in your bitcoin account and buy bitcoins using that money later or you can withdraw the money into your bank account. This will require a verification procedure. Alternatively you can use a service like OKPAY[25] which lets you easily cash your bitcoins.

Good Trading Practices

The process of selling/trading bitcoins is just like the process of trading stocks or derivatives. It has its own nuances and tricks of the trade. Here are some tips to help you trade better.

- Look out for group effects such as bandwagon effect[26] and herd mentality[27] while trading. Also study about other cognitive biases so that your behavior is affected the least by them.

- Always be a realist. Being optimistic is a good idea but ignoring negative trends will qualify as sheer stupidity. Be on top of information, scrutinize it with an open mind and then take decisions.

- Take other opinions into consideration. Even if you have confidence in your own forecasts, reading and pondering upon other conflicting reports will help you cover all bases and take an informed decision.

- Explore various ways of trading before sticking to one. This will let you find out the one which works the best for you.

---

25 OKPAY acts like a PayPal account. You can connect your OKPAY account to the exchange and withdraw funds to that account. The account will be linked to your bank account. Once the funds have been received in your OKPAY account, you can withdraw them to your bank account.
26 The bandwagon effect is a psychological phenomenon in which people do something primarily because other people are doing it, regardless of their own beliefs, which they may ignore or override. - Investopedia (http://www.investopedia.com/terms/b/bandwagon-effect.asp)
27 Herd mentality, or mob mentality, describes how people are influenced by their peers to adopt certain behaviors. - Wikipedia page (https://en.wikipedia.org/wiki/Herd_mentality)

Legality of the Currency

The currency is not legal in all countries. Before investing in bitcoins, it is important to understand if your country regulates it or has banned it. You can use the list published here https://en.wikipedia.org/wiki/Legality_of_bitcoin_by_country for this purpose.

It is not a wise idea to dabble into bitcoins if your government has declared it as an illegal currency.

Taxation and Government Claims on Bitcoin Income

For the governments that have declared bitcoins as legal, it is important to pay taxes on the income that you earn. The rules will differ from country to country and will be affected by the Income Tax Act in that country. Here are some general guidelines.

- **Received bitcoins for goods and services** - If you received bitcoins in exchange for providing goods or services, you will treat it like any other income received in dollars. For example, if you sold a box worth US$50 and accepted bitcoins for the same amount, US$50 will be considered as income and you will be required to pay tax on it.

- **Made profits by trading bitcoins** - If you traded bitcoins and made a profit on the trade, such profit will also be treated as income. You will be required to pay taxes on the profit. This assumes bitcoins to be similar to assets like gold and stocks.

- **Gross Income or Capital Gains** - In case you trade bitcoins, the income you earn will be included in capital gains. But in case you receive them for goods and services, the income will be included in gross income.

- **Bitcoins earned from mining** - If you mine bitcoins, the value of bitcoins when you mined them, is considered as income. You can deduct your expenses and pay taxes on the rest. If you sell your mined bitcoins, the profits that you make will also

Chapter 5: Selling and Trading Bitcoins

be considered income (capital gains) and you will have to pay taxes on it.

Again, an important point to note here is that the rules will differ from country to country. Before filing your taxes, please take a look at the rules in your country and proceed accordingly.

For example, the USA treats bitcoins as commodity and have tax provisions accordingly. Australia asks for GST (Goods and Services Tax) to be applied to sale and purchase of bitcoins. Bitcoins wouldn't be subject to VAT (Value Added Tax) in Europe.

To make the process easier for you and to record all transactions, you can use a bitcoin accounting and tax compliance software. Some notable ones in the area are Bitcoin Taxes (https://bitcoin.tax/), Libra Tax (http://www.libra.tech/) and Bit Prices (https://github.com/danda/bitprices).

Chapter 6 - Concerns and Risks

Bitcoin economy is comparatively new. And just like all things new, even the internet when it started, bitcoins are viewed with a certain sense of mystery and suspicion. There are many concerns that people have, when they want to start with bitcoins. A lot of these concerns are either unfounded or blown out of proportion. It is not being implied that bitcoin economy has no risks. No doubt, it has its own loopholes but they have to be studied and understood in context.

Common Concerns

Bitcoin is a slightly complicated system to understand for a layman. That is one reason why so many concerns are associated with it.

1) Bitcoins will be shut down by the government.

Because government doesn't directly controls bitcoins, a lot of people believe that it will eventually shut down bitcoins, disrupting the bitcoin economy and rendering the bitcoin holders with assets worth zero value.

While this is a theoretical possibility, it doesn't have many chances of happening. If the government decides to announce the currency as illegal or bans its use, the same ban will have to be continued for other cryptocurrencies. This has a very slim chance of happening as many corporations also use cryptocurrencies and they have the power to lobby against such a move.

Coming right down to the technicalities, it is impossible (in the literal sense) for governments to shut down bitcoin network because the government would be required to shut down the entire internet for that to plausibly happen. The government can, however, decide to shut all the bitcoin exchanges and exert pressure on entities to stop promoting bitcoins.

This will hurt bitcoin's reputation, maybe even devalue it a little but is still not enough to shut down the Bitcoin network in its entirety.

2) Bitcoin is on the internet and everything internet can be hacked.

Although the Bitcoin network is not completely secure and nothing ever can be, it is impressively secure. The entire Bitcoin network has built-in security mechanisms at every stage of the transaction to avoid fraud.

It starts with referencing of the inputs against the previous transactions, it continues with the use of blockchain technology and multiple checkpoints. The blockchain technology has been heralded as one of the most disruptive technologies. Many people even go to the extent of claiming that blockchain technology is here to stay, even if bitcoins don't.

Bitcoin, as a currency, is therefore safe.

But what's not safe are the wallets. Wallets have a chance of being hacked. Even exchanges have a chance of being hacked. This is very similar to credit card fraud and security concerns and shouldn't devalue bitcoin network as a whole.

3) Bitcoins aren't stable and cryptocurrencies are a fad.

It's true that the price of bitcoin experiences extreme volatility and it looks like a bubble waiting to be burst. While bitcoin isn't the most stable thing on the planet right now, it is here to stay. Cryptocurrencies have proved themselves to be the currencies of future. They solve a lot of problems faced by the traditional currencies and are secure at the same time.

The biggest risk that bitcoins will eventually face is from another cryptocurrency. While bitcoin is the most popular currency right now, there is still room for improvement in the realm of cryptocurrencies. A new currency which solves these concerns may benefit from the awareness that the Bitcoin network has generated and gain greater legitimacy.

Chapter 6: Concerns and Risks

Potential Risks

Each currency is faced with certain risks. In fact, risks are in-built and often inherent in most economic and financial institutions. Bitcoin is no different. There are a number of factors that threaten the autonomy, or in some cases security, of the Bitcoin network and therefore threaten to compromise the building blocks of bitcoins.

a) Concentration of mining power

Bitcoin network thrives on being a peer-to-peer and decentralized network. This is, in part, achieved by many nodes that confirm the bitcoin transactions. But with an increase in the specialized equipment for mining, mining has become unaffordable for a host of people who cannot afford to buy the expensive ASIC software. This has reduced the potential pool of mining candidates.

This has the capacity to undermine one of the core propositions of bitcoins - security through decentralization.

b) Bad apples

Bitcoin transactions are one-time transactions where no charge-back can take place. Moreover the transactions are anonymous (to a certain degree) and are not regulated. All good things, in theory. But the very fact has led to the Bitcoin network being used for illegal transactions or to circumspect the law.

This has also led to a lot of shady people using bitcoins to cover their tracks. Sometimes a few groups of people lose trust over a currency because of these reasons. But cash has been used in a similar fashion for years now.

While the kind of transactions isn't a cause for concern in itself for the average user, it may give the government a reason to outlaw bitcoins.

c) Greater downside for losses

The bitcoin network may be secure but the wallets, most certainly, aren't. They are susceptible to fraud and hacking.

On the surface, it doesn't seem like a huge problem. Credit cards are usually stolen for the purpose of fraud too. But the difference here is deregulation. If a credit card is stolen, the bank has enough authority to cancel the card and issue a new one.

d) Untraceable

Bitcoin transactions are completely untraceable. This means that it is impossible to acquire any meaningful information about the transaction once it has taken place. This may be a positive as well as a negative.

e) Speculative bubble

Many experts believe that bitcoins are bubbles waiting to be burst. This includes people like Alan Greenspan (a former Federal Reserve Chairman)[28], economists John Quiggin[29] and Robert Shiller (a Nobel Prize winner)[30]. Not only this, other experts regard bitcoins as a Ponzi scheme. The possibility of these forecasts coming true, or being believed by the followers, are major risks for bitcoins.

---

28 http://www.bloomberg.com/news/articles/2013-12-04/greenspan-says-bitcoin-a-bubble-without-intrinsic-currency-value

29 http://nationalinterest.org/commentary/the-bitcoin-bubble-bad-hypothesis-8353

30 http://www.nytimes.com/2014/03/02/business/in-search-of-a-stable-electronic-currency.html?_r=1

Chapter 7 - Conclusion

Despite all the risks, concerns and claims to the contrary, the popularity of bitcoins hasn't diminished one bit. A lot of big corporations as well as small sellers still accept bitcoins.

Does that mean you should also invest in bitcoins?

It depends. Before you start investing, it is important to understand a few things. First, it is impractical to put in all your hard-earned life savings in bitcoins. That is because the price of bitcoin is still very volatile. You could lose all your savings in a matter of minutes, theoretically. It is important to diversify and let bitcoins be just one of the many investments in your portfolio.

Second, it is possible and probable that another cryptocurrency can overtake bitcoins as the most legitimate cryptocurrency. In such a scenario, the price of bitcoins may plummet overnight leaving you with a bag full of currency with no value. Third, the governments could unite to overthrow bitcoins. This may or may not shut the network down but the price of bitcoin would definitely take a drop.

These are certain things to remember before you start investing in bitcoins and put all your savings in.

You could say that bitcoin is like a new kid on the block. You should definitely become friends with him but not at the cost of ditching your existing friends.

If you found this book helpful, please share a couple of sentences and a 4-5 star review on Amazon. It would mean a great deal to me and others who are considering purchasing this book.

If you have any questions or comments, feel free to email me at rj@notraceleft.com I try to reply to all questions that come in and that I am able to.

Thank you for reading **Bitcoin: The Ultimate Cryptocurrency Digital Money Guide**

Best of luck, and be informed!

R.J. Simmons

P.S. This book couldn't cover everything, but we know you now have enough information to make some informed choices with the future of your money.

Our wealth and privacy is constantly under attack and for all of my readers, I give you complimentary updates to the latest threats to your personal and financial information – with solutions and steps to take to protect yourself.

STAY connected by Subscribing to our FREE Newsletter:

www.NoTraceLeft.com

www.ingramcontent.com/pod-product-compliance
Lightning Source LLC
Chambersburg PA
CBHW060416190526
45169CB00002B/924